QUOTES FROM THE AUTHOR

"SPEND TIME ON CHANGE"

>>>>>

"THE CHANCE YOU TAKE IS

THE CHANCE YOU MAKE"

>>>>>

"BE YOUR BEST

BETTER"

THE
EFFECTS
OF
GLOBAL
WARMING

CISTA GIRL VEENUS GREEN ACTION HERO "The Effects of Global Warming" Library of Congress Cataloging-in-Publication Data includes a Glossary, and reader response engagement.
Library of Congress Control Number: PENDING
Publisher: KDP

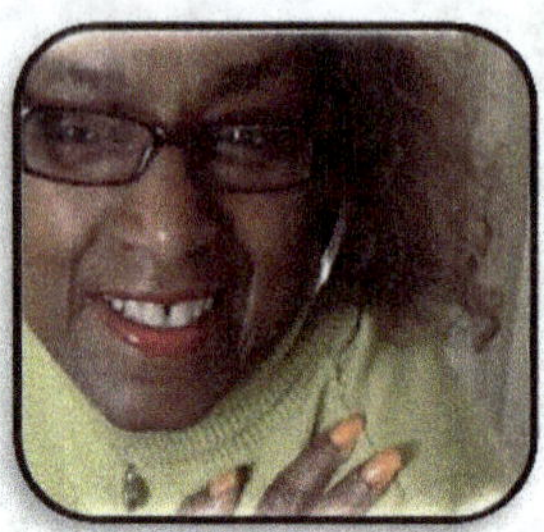

About the Author

Saundra Pope Pres., Founder, President
CISTA 4 CLEAN WATER INC.
Non-profit, 501c3
Environmental Corporation

Saundra Pope founded the CISTA 4 CLEAN WATER Corporation, with the commitment to heighten the awareness of the polluted state of our oceans and waterways, and the diminishing life on our planet, due to Global warming conditions. It was important to bring awareness of the healthy state of our planet to this generation so they can begin to build a healthier planet now and for future generations. The CISTA GIRL BEE FRIENDLY Environmental Club was formed. Our Global mission, "CISTA GIRLS leading the way to save our planet". Since the inception in 2016, Girls, 8-18 years old, became members of the CISTA GIRLS Environmental Club, and participated in numerous environmental projects, such as beach clean-ups, host TV shows, recycle projects, library presentations, and more, to educate the community on how to build a stronger relationship between man and the environment. Community service credits were awarded. This Book, CISTA GIRL VEENUS GREEN ACTION HERO was created to bring an awareness to the younger generation about GLOBAL WARMING and what they can do to reduce the conditions. The CISTA GIRL VEENUS GREEN ACTION HERO DOLL, will be manufactured to continue and provide hands on education about Global Warming and Climate Change. The acronym for C.I.S.T.A. C-commit to great health, I-invest in yourself, S-share with others,   T-team up for success, A-activate a positive plan. Please visit CISTA GIRLS "History at a Glance"www.cistagirlmagazine.com,   www.cistagirlsenvironmentalclub.com, www.cistagirlveenus.com, You Tube: CISTA GIRLS Environmental Club, Contact:cista4clanwater@gmail.com, cistagirveenus@gmail.com

THE
EFFECTS
OF
GLOBAL
WARMING

CISTA GIRL VEENUS GREEN ACTION HERO "The Effects of Global Warming" Library of Congress Cataloging-in-Publication Data includes a Glossary, and reader response engagement.
Library of Congress Control Number: PENDING
Publisher: KDP

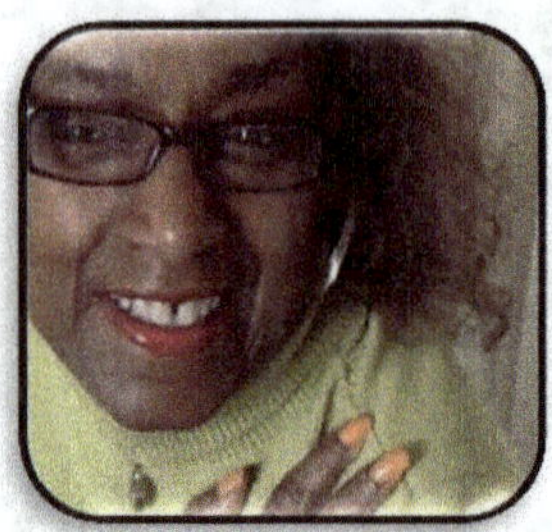

About the Author

Saundra Pope Pres., Founder, President
CISTA 4 CLEAN WATER INC.
Non-profit, 501c3
Environmental Corporation

Saundra Pope founded the CISTA 4 CLEAN WATER Corporation, with the commitment to heighten the awareness of the polluted state of our oceans and waterways, and the diminishing life on our planet, due to Global warming conditions. It was important to bring awareness of the healthy state of our planet to this generation so they can begin to build a healthier planet now and for future generations. The CISTA GIRL BEE FRIENDLY Environmental Club was formed. Our Global mission, "CISTA GIRLS leading the way to save our planet". Since the inception in 2016, Girls, 8-18 years old, became members of the CISTA GIRLS Environmental Club, and participated in numerous environmental projects, such as beach clean-ups, host TV shows, recycle projects, library presentations, and more, to educate the community on how to build a stronger relationship between man and the environment. Community service credits were awarded. This Book, CISTA GIRL VEENUS GREEN ACTION HERO was created to bring an awareness to the younger generation about GLOBAL WARMING and what they can do to reduce the conditions. The CISTA GIRL VEENUS GREEN ACTION HERO DOLL, will be manufactured to continue and provide hands on education about Global Warming and Climate Change. The acronym for C.I.S.T.A. C-commit to great health, I-invest in yourself, S-share with others,   T-team up for success, A-activate a positive plan. Please visit CISTA GIRLS "History at a Glance"www.cistagirlmagazine.com,   www.cistagirlsenvironmentalclub.com, www.cistagirlveenus.com, You Tube: CISTA GIRLS Environmental Club, Contact:cista4clanwater@gmail.com, cistagirveenus@gmail.com

TABLE OF CONTENTS

<table>
<tr><td></td><td>CHAPTERS</td><td>PAGE</td></tr>
</table>

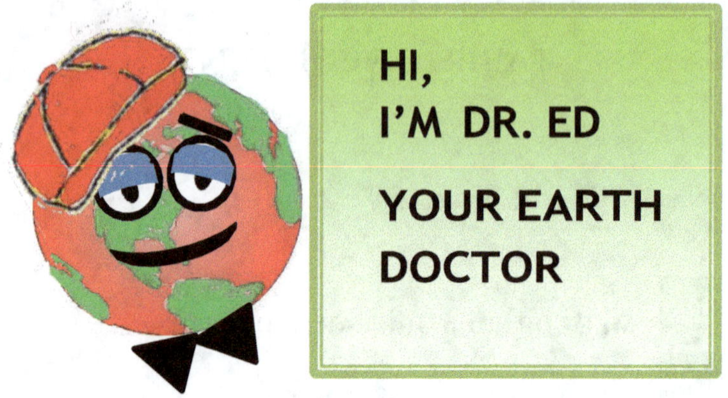

IT'S YOUR PLANET. WHATS GOING ON?

Life on Earth depends on energy coming from the sun. About half the light reaching Earth's atmosphere passes through the air and clouds to the surface, where it is absorbed and then radiated upward in the form of infrared heat. About 90 percent of this heat is then absorbed by the greenhouse gases and radiated back toward the surface, which is warmed to a life-supporting average of 59 degrees. This very helpful process is called the ***greenhouse effect***. The greenhouse effect, is caused by the interaction between Earth's atmosphere and incoming radiation from the sun.

TABLE OF CONTENTS

IT'S YOUR PLANET. WHATS GOING ON?

Life on Earth depends on energy coming from the sun. About half the light reaching Earth's atmosphere passes through the air and clouds to the surface, where it is absorbed and then radiated upward in the form of infrared heat. About 90 percent of this heat is then absorbed by the greenhouse gases and radiated back toward the surface, which is warmed to a life-supporting average of 59 degrees. This very helpful process is called the ***greenhouse effect***. The greenhouse effect, is caused by the interaction between Earth's atmosphere and incoming radiation from the sun.

WHAT
IS
GLOBAL
WARMING

WHAT IS GLOBAL WARMING?

Global warming is a gradual increase in the overall temperature of the earth's surface, oceans, and atmosphere, attributed to the greenhouse effect caused by increased levels of carbon monoxide, and other pollutants.

Global warming occurs when human activity introduces too much of certain types of gas into the atmosphere. More of this gas equals more warming. The atmospheric gases primarily responsible for the greenhouse effect are known as "greenhouse gases". They include water vapor, carbon monoxide, and methane gas. Hydrocarbon gases produced both through natural sources and human activities, include the decomposition of wastes in landfills, agriculture, and especially rice cultivation, as well as digestion and manure management associated with domestic livestock. The most dominant greenhouse gas is Carbon monoxide.

THE
CAUSE
OF
GLOBAL
WARMING

THE CAUSE OF GLOBAL WARMING

HUMANS CONTRIBUTE GREATLY TO GLOBAL WARMING

- OIL DRILLING
- GAS DRILLING
- METHANE GAS
- TRANSPORTATION
- FARMING
- DEFORESTATION
- FERTILIZERS
- PERMA FROST
- GARBAGE TRASH
- POWER PLANTS

WHAT IS PLASTIC POLLUTION?

8 million of those 300 million pieces of plastic is chucked into the sea annually – which is equivalent to dumping a garbage truck (1 ton) of plastic into the ocean per minute.

You know those crab legs you enjoy when you have a nice dinner out? Or escargot you splurge on? Or even that tilapia you regularly cook for dinner? And don't forget the tuna sandwiches you take for lunch. All of it will be more plastic than food as the years go by. Fish eat the plastic we divulge into the ocean. **By 2050, you'll be eating plastic every time you order seafood.** Plastic ocean pollution, a component of marine litter, injures and kills marine life, spreads toxins, and poses a potential threat to human health. Only a fraction of plastic ocean pollution is visible. Most of it consists of tiny degraded particles swirling in vast gyres spread across 16 million square kilometers of ocean surface, an area the size of the United States and Australia combined.

WHAT ARE POLLUTANTS FROM POWER PLANTS?

A **power plant** is an industrial facility that generates electricity from primary energy. Most **power plants** use one or more generators that convert mechanical energy into electrical energy in order to supply **power** to the electrical grid for society's electrical needs.

Coal run or **coal**-fired **power plants** burn **coal** to convert water into steam. This steam is then used to turn turbines which produces **electricity** with the help of a generator. Diesel-run and Natural Gas-run **power plants** are the other two **types** of thermal **power plants** that are commonly used for **electricity generation**.

Approximately 40% of global CO_2 emissions are emitted from **electricity generation** through the combustion of fossil fuels to **generate** heat needed to **power** steam turbines. Burning these fuels results in the **production** of **carbon dioxide** (CO_2)— the primary heat-trapping, "greenhouse gas" responsible for global warming.

WHAT ARE POLLUTANTS FROM OIL DRILLINGS?

Oil drilling a complex process that involves the drilling and pumping of oil from underground wells. **Oil drilling** is the process by which tubing is bored through the Earth's surface and a well is established. A pump is connected to the tube and the **petroleum** under the surface is forcibly removed from underground.

OFF SHORE OIL DRILLING Burn-off from the oil drilling industry impacts the carbon dioxide released into the atmosphere. Fossil fuel retrieval, processing and distribution accounts for roughly eight percent of carbon dioxide and thirty percent of methane pollution.

Drilling projects operate around the clock, disrupting wildlife, water sources, human health, recreation and other aspects of public lands that were set aside and held in trust for the American people.

WHAT ARE POLLUTANTS FROM GAS DRILLING?

DRILLING DISRUPTS WILDLIFE HABITATS

Oil and gas extraction is a menace to wildlife. Loud noises, human movement and vehicle traffic from drilling operations can disrupt natural species communication, breeding and nesting. The explosion of the Deepwater Horizon rig in the Gulf of Mexico in 2010, resulted in oil spill that covered 68,000 square mile of sea surface and killed approximately <u>1 million coastal and offshore seabirds, 5,000 marine mammals and 1,000 sea turtles</u>. These spills can have long-term environmental impacts and devastating effects on animals through direct contact, inhalation and ingestion of toxic chemicals. Oil and chemical spills can • Damage animals' liver, kidney, spleen, brain or other organs • Cause cancer, immune system suppression and reproductive failure   • Trigger long-term ecological changes by damaging animals' nesting or breeding grounds. There are <u>1.3 million</u> oil and gas facilities across the U.S.. More than 12 million people live within 1/2 mile of these facilities, and many are exposed to air and water pollution on a daily basis, The most affected are people of color, who typically <u>live in neighborhoods with</u> <u>more pollution</u>.

CARBON MONOXIDE POLLUTES THE EARTH

Carbon Monoxide colorless, odorless, and poisonous, is one of the six major air pollutants regulated in the United States and in many other nations around the world. When carbon-based fuels, such as coal, wood, and oil, burn incompletely or inefficiently, they produce carbon monoxide. The gas is spread by winds and circulation patterns throughout the lower atmosphere.

Carbon monoxide is a trace gas in the atmosphere, and it **does** not have a direct effect on the global temperature, like methane gas and **carbon dioxide do**. However, **carbon monoxide** plays a major role in atmospheric chemistry, and it affects the ability of the atmosphere to cleanse itself of many other polluting gases.

When **carbon monoxide is** emitted into the atmosphere it effects the amount of greenhouse gases, which **are** linked to climate change and **global** warming. This means that land and sea temperature increases changing to ecosystems, increasing storm activity and causing other extreme weather conditions.

The highest carbon monoxide concentrations occur around urban areas as a result of vehicle and industrial emissions.

WHAT IS CARBON DIOXIDE?

Carbon dioxide (chemical formula CO. 2) is a colorless gas with a density about 60% higher than that of dry air. **Carbon dioxide** occurs naturally in Earth's atmosphere as a trace gas.

An important trace gas in Earth's atmosphere. It is an integral part of the biogeochemical cycle in which carbon is exchanged between the Earth's oceans, soil, rocks and the biosphere.

According to EPA, in 2012, there is an unprecedented increase in CO2 in the atmosphere. CO2 accounted for about 82 percent of all United States greenhouse gas emissions (discharges). Carbon dioxide (CO2) absorbs infrared radiation heat and the global temperature increases. CO2 makes its way into earth's atmosphere through a variety of routes. For example, burning fossil fuels, releases CO2. Fossil fuel is a general term for buried combustible deposits of organic materials, formed from decayed plants and animals that have been converted to crude oil, coal, natural gas, or heavy oils by exposure to heat and pressure in the earth's crust over hundreds of millions of years. Fossil fuels can be burned, producing significant amounts of energy.

WHAT IS METHANE GAS?

METHNAE EMMISSIONS from live stock (COWS): When organic matter is broken down by bacteria under oxygen-starved conditions (decomposition) as in rice paddies, methane is produced. The process also takes place in the intestines of cows passing gas and with the increase in the amount of concentrated livestock production, the levels of methane released into the atmosphere is increasing. Industrial farming and ranching releases huge levels of methane and carbon dioxide into the atmosphere. Farming contributes forty percent of the methane and twenty percent of the carbon dioxide to worldwide emissions.

Methane is a chemical compound and is the main constituent of natural gas. The relative abundance of methane on Earth makes it an attractive fuel, although capturing and storing it poses challenges due to its gaseous state under normal conditions for temperature and pressure. Naturally occurring methane is found both below ground and under the seafloor, and is formed by both geological and biological processes.
Cattle are habitually cast as climate villains, responsible for 14.5 percent of human greenhouse gas emissions

HOW DOES TRANSPORTATION CONTRIBUTE TO GLOBAL WARMING?

Our personal vehicles are a major **cause** of **global warming**. Collectively, cars and trucks account for nearly one-fifth of all US emissions, emitting around 24 pounds of carbon dioxide and other **global-warming** gases for every gallon of gas.

About five pounds comes from the extraction, production, and delivery of the fuel, while the great bulk of heat-trapping emissions—more than 19 pounds per gallon—comes right out of a car's tailpipe.

Cars, trucks, planes, trains, ships, and freight produce nearly thirty percent of all US global warming emissions.

Global warming endangers our health, jeopardizes our national security, and threatens other basic human needs. Some impacts—such as record high temperatures, rising seas, and severe flooding and droughts—are already increasingly common.

FARMING CONTRIBUTES TO GLOBAL WARMING?

Global warming affects agriculture in a number of ways, including through changes in average temperatures, rainfall, and climate extremes (e.g., heat waves); changes in pests and diseases; changes in atmospheric carbon dioxide and ground-level ozone concentrations; changes in the nutritional quality of some foods;[and changes in sea level.

Climate change is already affecting agriculture, with effects unevenly distributed across the world. Future climate change will likely negatively affect crop production in low latitude countries, while effects in northern latitudes may be positive or negative.[Animal agriculture is also responsible for CO2 greenhouse gas production and a percentage of the world's methane, and future land infertility, and the displacement of local species.

Farming is not considered a part of climate change. Agriculture contributes to climate change both by anthropogenic emissions of greenhouse gases and by the conversion of non-agricultural land such as forests into agricultural land. Agriculture, forestry and land-use change contributed around 20 to 25% of global annual emissions in 2010.

WHAT IS DEFORESTATION?

Deforestation is one of the main contributors to climate change[1]. It comes in many forms: wildfire, agricultural clearcutting, livestock ranching, and logging for timber, among others. Forests cover 31% of the land area on Earth and annually 75,000 square kilometers (18.7 million acres) of the forest is lost. Mass deforestation continues to threaten tropical forests, their biodiversity and the ecosystem services they provide. The main area of concern of deforestation is in tropical rainforests since it is home to the majority of the biodiversity. **Deforestation** is the second largest anthropogenic source of carbon dioxide to the atmosphere, after fossil fuel combustion. Deforestation and forest degradation contribute to atmospheric greenhouse gas emissions through combustion of forest biomass and decomposition of remaining plant material and soil carbon. **Deforestation** is the second largest human-made source of carbon dioxide. When trees are killed, they release the carbon they have stored for photosynthesis and release nearly a billion tons of carbon into the atmosphere per year. Deforestation can contribute to the irreversible impact on natural habitat and thus threaten endangerment and even extinction of plant and animal.

FERTILIZERS AND GLOBAL WARMING

Excessive use of nitrogen-based **fertilizers** in agriculture is contributing **to** nitrous oxide emissions. Leftover nitrogen that hasn't been absorbed by plants, reacts with the soil **to** produce this dangerous greenhouse gas.

Fertilizers provide nutrients for plants. Nutrients needed in the largest quantities in agriculture are nitrogen, phosphorus and potassium. However, reducing **fertilizer** input can lead to reduced plant growth which can aggravate problems such as soil erosion.

Nitrogen

On farmed land, most nitrogen is in organic matter which must first be mineralized by soil microbes into ammonium or nitrate to be used by plants. Nitrate is easily leached from soil and so presents the most opportunity for pollution.

Environmental hazards, Groundwater pollution

Nitrate leaching through the soil can present a serious health hazard and contributes to soil acidification. When high rates of nitrogen are used or where clover grass pastures fix substantial nitrogen, especially on sandy or permeable soils, inevitably some nitrate is leached and may enter groundwater.

**GARBAGE
AND
TRASH**

TRASH AND GLOBAL WARMING

Toxic **waste** materials **can** contaminate surface water, groundwater, soil, and air which causes more problems for humans, other species, and ecosystems. **Waste** treatment and disposal produces significant green house gas (GHG) emissions, notably methane, which are contributing significantly to **global warming**. The surface temperature of the Earth has risen in the past century, The life cycle of a product both directly and indirectly contributes to the emission of greenhouse gases into the atmosphere and affects the global climate. The manufacturing of products affects greenhouse gas emissions directly through the manufacturing process itself, while it indirectly affects emissions from the energy produced while running the manufacturing plant, including the carbon dioxide released from gasoline-powered vehicles to transport the product, and the release of methane gas during the decomposition of the product when it is discarded in a landfill.

THE
EFFECTS
OF
GLOBAL
WARMING

MAJOR EFFECTS OF GLOBAL WARMING

More than 1,500,000 people die from climate change-related diseases on a yearly basis. Changes in weather conditions can lead to health conditions ranging from heat-related heart and respiratory problems to malaria. Droughts, floods and warmer temperatures create a habitat for insects and creatures such as mosquitoes and other disease-carrying agents. Diseases like west nile virus, cholera, lyme disease and dengue fever which were earlier considered to be confined to tropical areas are now spreading worldwide due to the globally rising temperatures.

NATION'S ECONOMY:

Natural disasters such as hurricanes and floods as an effect of the global warming process, end up becoming a costly affair for the government in terms of clean-up costs, property damage and rehabilitation costs a hike in food and energy costs.

Crisis like this can result in Diminishing Water Supplies. If these water shortages are persistent, it will cause a major disruption in global food production by affecting agriculture and paving a way for starvation.

WHAT IS PERMA FROST?

PERMA FROST a thick subsurface layer of soil that remains frozen throughout the year, occurring chiefly in polar regions The melting of permafrost releases tons of trapped green house gases which furthers speeds up the melting of more permafrost. It **is** thought that **permafrost** thawing could exacerbate **global warming** by releasing methane and other hydrocarbons, which **are** powerful greenhouse gases. It also could encourage erosion because **permafrost** lends stability to barren Arctic slopes.

GLOBAL WARMING CONTRIBUTES TO VIOLENT HURRICANES

Hurricanes are more intense. They get their energy from the temperature difference between the warm tropical ocean and the cold upper atmosphere.

Rise in temperature: North America reached record highs in 2012, making it the hottest year since record keeping began in 1895.   Ocean water will expand contributing to the rise in sea level. Warmer temperatures and warmer ocean waters would fuel the intensity of storms, leading to a high number of devastating hurricanes. Dorian, the second strongest Atlantic hurricane in modern record, is a prime example of storms reaching the highest category on the Saffir-Simpson hurricane scale. Climate change is worsening the impact of storms like Hurricane Dorian, with higher storm surges, increased rainfall and rising storm intensity.

Storm surge, not wind or rain, is the number one killer in hurricanes, and climate change is making it worse. Storm surge is the rise in ocean levels brought about by the wind and low pressure in a hurricane. When the winds blow onshore, it pushes the water higher, forcing it farther inland than normal tidal levels.

GLOBAL WARMING EFFECTS ON CORAL REEFS

The 'bleaching' of corals from small but prolonged rises in sea temperature is a severe danger for ocean ecosystems, and many other species in the oceans as they rely on coral reefs for their survival. Climate change is the greatest global threat to coral reef ecosystems. Scientific evidence now clearly indicates that the Earth's atmosphere and ocean are warming, and that these changes are primarily due to greenhouse gases derived from human activities.

As temperatures rise, mass coral bleaching events and Infectious disease outbreaks are becoming more frequent. Additionally, carbon dioxide absorbed into the ocean from the atmosphere has already begun to reduce calcification rates in reef-building and reef-associated organisms by altering seawater chemistry through decreases in pH. This process is called ocean acidification. Climate change will affect coral reef ecosystems, through sea level rise, changes to the frequency and intensity of tropical storms, and altered ocean circulation patterns. When combined, all of these impacts dramatically alter ecosystem function, as well as the goods and services coral reef ecosystems provide to people around the globe.

PLANTS

Plants and animals: Live in regions with extremely specific climate and geological conditions, such as temperature and rainfall patterns, that enable them to survive and reproduce. Any change in the climate of the specific habitat can affect the plants and animals that exist there, as well as the overall makeup of the environment.

Up to half of plant and animal species in the world's most naturally rich areas, such as the Amazon and the Galapagos, could face local extinction by the turn of the century due to climate change if carbon emissions continue to rise unchecked.

"Hotter days, longer periods of drought, and more intense storms are becoming the new normal, and species around the world are already feeling the effects

THE POLAR BEAR FAMILY SEARCHING FOR NEW HOMES

The polar bear is considered to be an endangered species whose numbers are falling because of their inability to adapt to the volatile temperature changes in the Polar Regions. Montana's Glacier National Park, where about 150 glaciers were once located, only 25 glaciers remain, according to the U.S. Geological Survey (USGS) Glaciers, polar ice shelves and other ice bodies to completely destabilize and melt. This in turn increases the amount of water in the world's oceans thus contributing to a rise in sea levels. This rise especially threatens populations located in low-lying coastal areas because of their higher vulnerability to flooding. Scientists speculate that the melting ice from Greenland and Antarctica is capable of rising the sea level to more than 20 feet. Climate change is expected to have the most severe impact on water supplies. "Water shortages in the future are likely to threaten food production, reduce sanitation, and hinder economic development and damage ecosystems.

CRYSTAL PRODUCTION

Methane emissions from ice crystals: Another source of methane is "methane clathrate: a compound containing large amounts of methane trapped in the crystal structure of ice. As methane escapes from the Arctic seabed, the rate of global warming will increase significantly.

Scientists at the Department of Energy's Oak Ridge National Laboratory have found a simple, reliable process to capture carbon dioxide directly from ambient air, offering a new option for carbon capture and storage strategies to combat global warming.

Initially, the ORNL team was studying methods to remove environmental contaminants such as sulfate, chromate or phosphate from water. To remove those negatively charged ions, the researchers synthesized a simple compound known as guanidine designed to bind strongly to the contaminants and form insoluble crystals that are easily separated from water.

In the process, they discovered a method to capture and release carbon dioxide that requires minimal energy and chemical input.

RISE IN SEA LEVELS WORLD WIDE DISPLACE GENERATIONAL CULTURES

Scientists predict an increase in sea levels world wide due to the melting of two massive ice sheets in Antarctica and Greenland. The effects of rising sea levels, will displace millions of people. When **sea levels rise** it can have devastating **effects** on coastal habitats farther inland, it can cause destructive erosion, wetland flooding, aquifer and agricultural soil contamination with salt, and lost habitat for fish, birds, and plants.

RISE IN SEA LEVELS WILL SEEP INTO THE FRESHWATER SOURCES in the ground that many coastal areas rely on for their drinking water. These underground water sources, called aquifers, are crucial springs of freshwater. Groundwater accounts for most of the planet's freshwater. Saltwater is unsafe to drink. Those same freshwater sources we use for drinking also supply the water we use for irrigation. Saltwater can stunt or even kill crops. Pumping freshwater from the ground for human use contributes to a rise in sea levels.

VOLCANIC ERUPTIONS

VOLCANOES EFFECTED BY GLOBAL WARMING

Tens of thousands of people have evacuated their land in Bali as the nearby volcano Mount Agung angrily spits ash and its magma rises. Many Balinese hold the mountain sacred and accept its occasional outbursts as moral admonishments whereas geologists consider this activity a routine part of Earth's behavior. But scientists have found another force—climate change—affects the frequency of eruptions. Now a new study shows even relatively minor climate variations may have such an influence. If they are right, today's global warming could mean more and bigger volcanic eruptions in the future.

Throughout its history Earth has gone through periods of massive natural climate change such as entering and leaving ice ages. Scientists have noted volcanic eruptions tended to increase as glaciers melted. In a recent study published in *Geology* researchers looked at smaller-scale changes in glacial coverage to see if these incremental differences had any effect.

MORE HURRICANES

Over the past century, the number of hurricanes that strike each year has more than doubled. Scientists blame global warming and the rising temperature of the surface of the seas.

MORE FLOODS

During the summer of 2007, Britain suffered its worst flood in 60 years. Scientists point the finger directly at global warming, which changed precipitation patterns and is now causing more "intense rainstorms across parts of the northern hemisphere."

MORE FIRES

Hotter temperatures could also mean larger and more devastating wildfires. This past summer in California, a blaze consumed more than 33,500 acres, or 52 square miles.

MORE DANGEROUS LIGHTENING

NASA scientists now say as the world gets hotter, even smaller thunderstorms will pose more severe risks with "deadly lightning, damaging hail and the potential for tornadoes."

MORE HIGHER SEA LEVELS

Scientists believe sea levels will be three feet higher by the end of the century than they are now.

MORE MOLD AND RAGWEED = MORE ALLERGIES, ASTHMA

A Harvard Study in 2004 showed higher concentrations of CO2 in the atmosphere producing more mold and ragweed, producing higher rates of asthma attacks, especially in kids.

MORE STARVATION

A study by IISS found that reduced water supplies and hotter temperatures mean "65 countries were likely to lose over 15 percent of their agricultural output by 2100."

MORE LARGE-SCALE MIGRATIONS

Global warming will turn already-dry environments into deserts, causing the people who live there to migrate in massive numbers to more livable places.

MORE VANISHING LAKES

What happened to the five-acre glacial lake in Southern Chile? In March, it was there. In May, it was … gone. Scientists blame global warming.

MORE OCEANS ARE TURNING TO ACID

Oceans absorb CO2 which, when mixed with seawater. turns to a weak carbonic acid.

MORE GREEN GRASS IN ANTARCTICA

Grass has started to grow in Antarctica in areas formerly covered by ice sheets and glaciers.

MORE GREENLAND'S MELTING

Greenland is melting at a rate of 52 cubic miles per year. If Greenland's entire 2.5 million cubic kilometers of ice were to melt, it would lead to a global sea level rise of 7.2

MORE MOSQUITOES

Mosquitoes like to live in drains and sewer puddles. During long dry spells (brought on by higher temperatures) these stagnant pools become a vital source of water for thirsty birds and mosquitoes. At the same time, these dry spells "reduce the populations of dragonflies, lacewings, and frogs that eat the mosquitoes." Increased CO2 levels cause poison ivy and other weeds to grow "taller, lusher, and more resilient."

GOODBYE TO THE MANGROVE TREES

Rising sea levels linked to climate change mean we could lose half of the mangrove trees of the Pacific Isles by the end of the century.

SAY GOODBYE TO THE GREAT BARRIER REEF

According to the U.N., the Great Barrier Reef will disappear within decades as "warmer, more acidic seas could severely bleach coral in the world-famous reef as early as 2030."

SAY FAREWELL TO GLACIERS

"In Glacier National Park, the number of glaciers in the park has dropped from 150 to 26 since 1850.

DYING GRAY WHALES

Global warming is thwarting majestic gray whales' struggle to recover from their endangered status. In recent years, more gray whales have been washing up on beaches after starving to death. Rising ocean temps, are killing off their food supply.

DEATH MARCH OF THE PENGUINS

Scientists blame global warming for the declining penguin population, as warmer waters and smaller ice floes force the birds to travel further to find food. "Emperor penguins … have dropped from 300 breeding pairs to just nine in the western Antarctic Peninsula."

FAREWELL TO FROGS

An estimated two-thirds of the 110 known species of Harlequin frog in Central and South America have vanished since the 1980s due to the outbreak of a deadly frog fungus, brought on by global warming.

FAREWELL TO THE WALRUS

Walrus pups rest on sea ice while their mothers hunt for food. A new study shows more and more abandoned pups are being stranded on floating islands as ice islands melt.

SAY GOODBYE TO GUACAMOLE

Scientists from the Lawrence Livermore National Laboratory predict hotter temps will cause a 40 percent drop in California's avocado production over the next 40 years.

SAY GOODBYE TO MIXED NUTS

Scientists from the Lawrence Livermore National Laboratory predict hotter temps will cause a 20 percent drop in California's almond and walnut crops over the next 40 years.

SAY GOODBYE TO FRENCH FRIES

Scientists from the Consultative Group on International Agricultural Research say warmer temperatures are killing off wild relatives of potato and peanut plants, "threatening a valuable source of genes necessary to help these food crops fight pests and drought."

SAY GOODBYE TO SALMON DINNERS

Wild pacific salmon have already vanished from 40 percent of their traditional habitats in the Northwest and the NRDC warns warmer temperatures are going to erase 41 percent of their habitat by 2090.

SAY GOODBYE TO LOBSTER DINNERS

Lobsters thrive in the chilly waters of New England, but recent numbers show that as those waters have warmed up, "the big-clawed American lobster has been withering at an alarming rate from New York state to Massachusetts."

SAY GOODBYE TO SNORKELING VACATIONS

The elkhorn coral which used to line the floor of
the Caribbean are nearly gone, "victims of pollution, warmer
water and acidification from the greenhouse gas carbon dioxide
seeping into oceans."

SAY GOODBYE TO
THAT TROPICAL ISLAND VACATION

Indonesia's environment minister announced this year that
scientific studies estimate about 2,000 of the country's lush
tropical islands could disappear by 2030 due to rising sea levels.

SAY GOODBYE TO BASEBALL

The future of the ash tree—from which all baseball bats are
made—is in danger of disappearing, thanks to a combination of
killer beetles and global warming.

SAY GOODBYE TO CHRISTMAS TREES

The Pine Bark Beetle, which feeds on and kills pine trees, used
to be held in control by cold winter temperatures. Now the
species is thriving and killing off entire forests in British
Columbia.

SAY GOODBYE TO LIGHT AND DRY WINES AND
PINOT NOIR

Warmer temperatures mean grapes
In California and France develop their sugars too quickly. As a
result, growers are forced to either a) leave the grapes on the
vines longer, which dramatically raises the alcoholic content of
the fruit or b) pick the grapes too soon and make overly sweet
wine that tastes like jam. Warmer temperatures are damaging the
pinots from Oregon "baking away" the grape's berry flavors.

HOW
TO
REDUCE
GLOBAL
WARMING

40

HOW
TO
REDUCE
GLOBAL
WARMING

THIS IS HOW YOU CAN REDUCE
GLOBAL WARMING CONDITIONS

CONSERVE WATER

Conserve water at home. The average family of four in the U.S. uses about 400 gallons of water every day. Wasting water is one of the biggest ways individuals impact the health of the planet. Taking measures to use less water is something you can start doing right away.

CHECK OFF AS MANY ITEMS AS POSSIBLE.

Check and fix any water leaks.
Install water-saving devices on your faucets and toilets.
Don't wash dishes with the water running continuously.
Replace old toilets with new ones that use a lot less water.
Wash and dry only full loads of laundry and dishes.
Don't use too much water to wash the lawn.
Don't leave the faucet running while you brush your teeth.
Take shorter showers instead of baths.

USE FEWER CHEMICALS

Chemicals used to wash our bodies, homes, cars and everything else get washed down the drain or absorbed in the grass, and eventually end up in the water supply. Chemicals are polluting our waterways, diminishing our eco system and contaminating our drinking water.
Use a solution of 1/2 cup white vinegar and 1/2 cup water, instead of using chemical-laden shampoos and soaps. Try making your own.

Instead of using pesticides hire a GREEN company to get rid of weeds/pests.

Dispose of toxic waste the right way. Paint, motor oil, ammonia, and a host of other chemicals. They should not be poured down the drain or directly into the ecosystem. They'll soak into the earth and end up in the groundwater (drinking water).Contact your local sanitation department to find out about best practice for disposing of hazardous waste and toxic chemicals.

STOP OCEAN POLLUTION

Water pollution arrives from dumping plastic and other debris into our oceans and waterways. Plastic water bottles is the biggest polluter dumping tons of plastic bottles yearly with 500 years to decompose.

Help identify water polluters. In order to protect the earth's water, concerned citizens should speak up and find ways to stop pollution at its source.

Join a local environmental group that works to clean up the water ways in your area, whether it's a river, lake, beach or ocean. Contact cista4cleanwater@gmail.com.

Contact your local representative to speak up about your views on keeping drinking water chemical-free.

Volunteer to help clean up beaches or riverbanks.

Help others get involved in efforts to clean up the eco systems in your area.

USE LESS ELECTRICITY

If every American household replaced one regular lightbulb with a C.F.L., (compact florescence lightbulb) the rate of pollution reduction would be equivalent to removing one million cars from the road. A 30-watt C.F.L. produces about as much light as an ordinary 100-watt bulb.

Use solar power for home and water heating.

Shut off electrical equipment in the evening when you leave work.

If you have central air conditioning, do not close vents in unused rooms.

Lower the thermostat on your water heater to 120.

Turn down or shut off your water heater when you will be away for extended periods.

When using an oven, minimize door opening while it is in use; it reduces oven temperature by 25 to 30%.

Clean the lint filter in your dryer after every load so that it uses less energy.

Plant trees to shade your home.

Replace old windows with energy efficient ones.

Insulate your home as best as you can.

Unplug devices when possible. Leaving devices plugged in, such as laptop chargers or toasters, can use "phantom" energy. Even when an appliance is turned off, it may still use power. Use a power strip to turn lots of things off with the flip of a single switch.

Don't use electronic exercise machines. Use a real bicycle (or a unicycle), or walk to get to nearby destinations or for pleasure. Calisthenics, push-ups, Zumba, and other bodyweight exercises work, as well.

Drive a hybrid car. If you have been looking for a new vehicle, consider buying a hybrid car. These kinds of cars, which run on both gasoline and electric motors, are rapidly becoming more popular and available in different models. They not only give off less emissions into the air, they also can save you money with fewer trips to the gas station. You may also be able to get a tax credit on your federal taxes during the tax year that you bought a hybrid.

Get an Electric Lawn Mower. Surrender your gas lawn mower. Gasoline lawn mowers are among the dirtiest of modern machines. A study found that using a four-horsepower lawn mower for an hour causes the same amount of pollution as driving a car 93 miles.

The trouble with gas lawn mowers is that they not only emit CO2, they are also responsible for releasing carcinogens such as polycyclic aromatic hydrocarbons into the air.

GREEN GRILLING

If you have a charcoal barbecue grill, make sure your charcoal comes from a sustainable source. Enormous areas of tropical rainforest are destroyed every year to produce the 900,000 tons of charcoal.

SWITCH TO GREEN POWER

Get your electricity from renewable energy sources such as wind, sun, water, biomass, or solar power. The leading cause of industrial air pollution is electricity production. According to the American Lung Association, more than 50,000 Americans die each year from air/pollution-related causes. If available, get your electricity from renewable energy sources such as wind, sun, water, and biomass, all of which generate electricity with fewer environmental impacts.

BUY LOCAL GOODS

Buying local helps combat global warming in two ways. You don't have to travel as far to get what you need, and products don't have to travel as far to get to you, either. Making smart choices about where your food, clothes, and other goods come from can help make a dent in global warming.
Shop at farmer's markets and buy food that was produced as close to your home as possible.
When you're online shopping, pay attention to how far the items you order will travel before they arrive. Try to find items that won't have to travel long distances.

Pay attention to where your clothes, electronics, home goods, and other possessions were made. As much as possible, buy items that were made in your region.

REUSED ITEMS

Buy second hand clothes and other items from thrift stores. Donate household items, and turn useless junk into jewelry, or reusable fabric bags.
Many communities have banned stores from giving out plastic bags, move into using reusable bags.

EAT MORE VEGETABLES

Eat vegetables and locally-sourced meat. Industrial farming practices are not only harmful to individual animals, they're unsafe for the planet itself. Factory farming produces a lot of air and water pollution, a major contribution to global warming. You can address this issue in a personal way by doing the following:
Eat more vegetables. This simple change is a way of opting out of the factory farming industry.
Go Vegetarian One Day a Week.
To produce one pound of beef requires 2,500 gallons of water—that's 40 times more water than is used to produce a pound of potatoes. Before buying beef, think about the immense cost of energy used to raise cattle and to transport **meat to your supermarket shelf. Besides all this, cows** consume enormous amounts of antibiotics and are a major source of methane, (passing gas) which is the number-two greenhouse gas.
Meat and dairy production is highly resource-intensive and inefficient. Attempting vegetarianism or veganism is definitely one of the best things you can do for the environment and also for your health

MEATLESS MONDAY

Meatless Monday is a national non-profit public health campaign that encourages people to give up meat one day a week.

DRINK SHADE GROWN COFFEE

According to coffeeresearch.org, about 150 species of birds live on shade-grown-coffee farms. With increased demand for cheap coffee, many Latin American growers have moved toward full-sun plantations, clearing the habitat of numerous native birds and increasing the use of pesticides and fertilizers. By drinking shade-grown coffee, you can help bird habitats and reduce the need for farming chemicals. Shade-grown coffee beans can be purchased at many grocery stores. Or ask.

AVOID PALM OIL

Palm oil is collected from oil palms in parts of Indonesia and Africa and is the number one cause of rainforest deforestation. Check the ingredients of your food and cosmetics; avoid companies that export large amounts of palm oil.

HELP SAVE HONEY BEES

You can help save the environment by helping to save honey bees and other insects which make a huge contribution to our world. The diminishing and disappearance of bees is potentially devastating to agriculture and most plant life. Find out how you can save honey bees

MINI CUPS

Billions of mini cups of ground coffee were sold in 2014, and the number of cups that ended up in landfills could circle the earth 12 times. Find a way.
Use a mug or other reusable cups for your coffee instead of a disposable cup.

DRINKING WATER

Use reusable bottles for your drinking water. Buying bottled water is unnecessary when you have a quality water filter. Buy your water filter system to avoid plastic bottle dumping. Request a water quality report from your city. Use their enclosed water test kit to test your water quality.

BEST WATER FILTER

A powerful water filter is highly recommended.
Carry your water bottle with you. Be in control of the quality of water you drink. More details at www.cista4cleanwater.com

PROTECTING THE LAND

Try making these changes:
Produce less waste. Everything you throw in the garbage, tie up and take out to be collected is going to end up in a landfill. Plus, all that trash - plastic, paper, metal, and whatnot was likely manufactured using unsustainable practices that hurt the health of the earth's land. By making less trash, you can reduce the impact on GLOBAL WARMING.

RESUEABLE PRODUCTS

Buy products that you can reuse. Get glass containers instead of flimsy plastic ones.
Don't use plastic bags - use cloth.

CIGARETTE BUTTS DISCARD THEM PROPERLY

About 4.5 trillion cigarette butts are littered worldwide each year—making them the most-littered item. Filters decompose, they release harmful chemicals that enter the earth's land and water during the decaying process. There is nothing earth-friendly about the breakdown. If you must smoke, carry something to store your used butts in until you can discard them properly, in the GARBAGE.

AVOID PLASTIC BAGS

Americans use 84 billion plastic bags annually, a considerable contribution to the 500 billion to one trillion used worldwide. Made from polyethylene, plastic bags are not biodegradable and are making their way into our oceans and waterways. According to recent studies, the oceans are full of tiny fragments of plastic that are beginning to work their way up the food chain. There are islands of plastic as large as Texas floating in our oceans today. Plastic bags take 500 years to decompose. More details at www.cista4cleanwater.com Avoid plastic bags.

MAINTAIN AND REPAIR DURABLE STUFF INSTEAD OF BUYING NEW ONES

Avoid products with several layers of packaging when only one is sufficient. About 33% of what we throw away is packaging.

Use reusable plates and utensils instead of disposable ones. Use reusable containers to store food instead of aluminum foil and cling wrap.

Buy rechargeable batteries for devices used frequently.

Copy and print on both sides of paper.

Reuse items like envelopes, folders and paper clips.

Use e-mail or texting as a substitute for paper correspondence.

Use recycled paper.

Mend clothes instead of buying new ones.

Buy used furniture.

MAKE YOUR OWN STUFF

Make your own stuff. When you make your own dinner from scratch or mix up your own cleaning supplies, you naturally make less waste. Single-sized TV dinners, shampoo bottles and the like can really add up in the trash can! Here are a few things you can make on your own:

Buy ingredients in bulk to cut back on packaging.

Body products. Shampoo, conditioner, lotion, toothpaste etc., you can make it! Try replacing a few things at first, then work up to making most of what you use. Tip: coconut oil is a brilliant replacement for lotion, deep conditioner and face wash.

Cleaning products. Everything from window cleaner to bathroom cleaner to oven cleaner can be made using all-natural supplies.

BUILD A HEALTHY YARD

Compost. This is an excellent way to cut back on waste and improve the health of the land. Instead of throwing your food scraps in the trash, compost them in a bin or a pile. After tending the pile for a few weeks, you'll have rich soil you can spread on your grass or use to make a delicious vegetable garden. Plant a garden. Create a garden plot with vegetables, fruits, and/or herbs.

NO FERTILIZER

Try to implement techniques so that your garden does not require fertilizers or excessive watering. For example, adding mulch to your garden will seal in water and make the soil moist.
Avoid pesticides, herbicides, and man-made chemical fertilizers. Pesticides kill hundreds of birds and other animals per year. If you have unwanted weeds, pull or hoe them out yourself, clip them down, or plant a ground cover in their place. Contact a Green Company.
Check out permaculture, integrative pest management, poly-cropping, and other techniques to reduce or eliminate the need for chemical pesticides and fertilizer.
Ensure that excess fertilizer is not washed into storm drains or waterways.

PLANT A TREE

Plant a tree. Add a tree to your yard. Trees absorb carbon dioxide and emit oxygen, and they also improve area water quality and help make the ground more fertile for other plants.
Ditch your noisy electric- or gas-powered leaf blower and use a rake to gather up leaves or other debris in your yard.
Use a broom instead of a hose to clean dirt from a paved area.
Plant trees and don't cut them. Trees protect land from getting eroded, and they're an integral part of the ecosystem. In saving trees you'll be protecting not only land, but water and air, too.

If you have room in your yard, consider planting a few
trees to invest in the future of your neighborhood.
Do research to figure out what trees will be most
beneficial to the environment where you live. Plant native
species.
Aim to plant trees that will grow tall and provide shade.

CONSERVING ENERGY

Use a solar powered outdoor light. These lights come
with rechargeable batteries that are charged by the sun
during the day.
Install skylights and solar tubes. Skylights and solar tubes
are installed in your ceiling and are designed to let in
more light. This will reduce the electricity you need to
light your house. Some types can even convert sunlight
into electricity.
Maintain your appliances, and choose energy-efficient
appliances if you are purchasing new ones.
Clean the coils on your refrigerator about once a year.
Clean the vent on your clothes dryer about once a year.
Clean the lint filter each time you use the dryer.
Invest in SOLAR panels. A home utility bill can drop by
20% with the use of converted solar energy.

RECYCLE ALL YOU CAN

If you have curbside recycling, use it. Be sure to separate
your recycling into glass, metal, paper and so on.
Avoid using disposable items. Anything you use only a
few times and throw away   consumes resources
only to spend centuries in a landfill.
Use rechargeable batteries instead of disposable batteries.
Batteries not only take up landfill space, as they can't be
incinerated. They also can leak acid into the Earth.
Dispose properly of hazardous waste. Many materials,
including batteries, fluorescent light bulbs, e-waste (most
anything with batteries or a plug), cleaning products,
pharmaceuticals, pesticides, automotive fluids, and paint,

should never be disposed of in a landfill, sanitary sewer, or storm sewer. Instead, contact your city for proper disposal opportunities. Use a washable cloth or sponge for most of your kitchen cleanup instead of paper towels.

For the paper products you do use, look for products made from 80-100% recycled paper, preferably with a high post-consumer content.

For most household cleaning, look for reusable terry cleaning cloths. They are inexpensive, especially when bought in bulk, and can be washed and reused hundreds of times.

Consider using cloth diapers. keep potentially dangerous chemicals away from your baby's skin, and do a good thing for the planet as well.

Stop your junk mail from coming. If you get several catalogs which you do not need, call and ask them to stop sending them to you.

To stop unwanted credit card solicitations for either 5 years or permanently. Sign up at (https://www.optoutprescreen.com)

RECYCLE GLASS

Recycle glass (think beer bottles, jars, juice containers) either through curbside programs or at community drop-off centers. Glass takes more than one million years to decompose; Americans generate almost 13 million tons of glass waste a year. Glass produced from recycled glass reduces related air pollution by 20 percent and related water pollution by 50 percent.

GREEN PAINT

GO GREEN PAINT. Most paint is made from petrochemicals, and its manufacturing process can create 10 times its own weight in toxic waste. It also releases volatile organic compounds (V.O.C.'s) that threatens public health. It evaporates, allowing paint to dry quickly.) They cause photochemical reactions in the atmosphere, leading to ground-level smog that can cause eye and skin irritation, lung and breathing problems, headaches, nausea, and nervous-system and kidney damage. The best alternative? Natural paints.

BUY LOCALLY.
GIGANTIC COST, IN FOOD TRANSPORTATION
Food is traveling farther than ever. Once upon a time people ate seasonally—artichokes in the winter, cherries in June. Now you can buy most fruits and vegetables practically year-round. The average American meal contains ingredients produced in at least five other countries. The transportation of food and agricultural products constitutes more than 20 percent of total commodity transport within the U.S. To help reduce CO_2 emissions (released from trucks, airplanes, and cargo ships), it's best to buy food that's in season, organic, and grown locally.

ENVIRONMENTAL ISSUES

Use the news media and social media to highlight environmental issues.

CISTA GIRL VEENUS GREEN ACTION HERO

"GO GREEN" projects and programs will help reduce GLOBAL Warming and Climate change conditions.

Cista Girl
VEENUS
GREEN ACTION HERO
LEAD THE WAY
SAVE THE PLANET
RECYCLE
SUSTAIN-ABILITY
LESS TRASH
SAVE WATER
MAKE REUSEABLE BAGS
REDUCE PLASTIC DUMPING
CISTA GIRL VEENUS GREEN ACTION HERO SAYS "GO GREEN"

Hello, my name is CISTA GIRL VEENUS GREEN ACTION HERO. My name was adopted from the planet "VENUS" the second planet from the Sun, named after the Roman goddess of love and beauty. I am an Environmental, Empowerment and Education DOLL with the mission to Educate the community about the cause and effects of GLOBAL WARMING and how they can be engaged to reduce the impact of Global warming and Lead the way to save the planet, now and for future generations.

My "GO GREEN" PLANET RESCUE MISSION will help build health and wellness and a healthy plant too. "GO GREEN" means to live a lifestyle that is healthy for the environment and build health and wellness for yourself. The next few pages will give examples of my "GO GREEN" Planet Rescue Mission. To learn more about CISTA GIRL VEENUS, visit the website: www.cistagirlveenus.com. CISTA GIRL VEENUS GREEN ACTION HERO is powered by CISTA 4 CLEAN WATER, a 501c3, Non Profit, Corporation. Saundra Pope, Pres., Founder and the creator of CISTA GIRL VEENUS GREEN ACTION HERO DOLL.

**LEAD THE WAY TO SAVE THE PLANET.
CHOOSE ANY OF THE "GO GREEN"
INITIATIVES AND SHARE WITH OTHERS.**

MAKE RE-USEABLE BAGS Plastic bags end up in oceans and landfills that contaminate waterways and groundwater.

START YOUR WINDOW SILL GARDEN. Be in control of the pesticides used on your Vegetables Eat healthy build a healthy planet.

EAT MORE VEGGIES

Eating a Veggie diet means 2.5 x less carbon emissions than a meat based diet.

RECYCLE

Recycle helps break waste items down into their raw materials, which are then used to re-make new items. **Helps reduce dumping in Landfills.**

SINGLE USE BOTTLES

DUMPED INTO LANDFILLS that seep into waterways and groundwater. Groundwater is drinking water.

PLANTS FOR CLEAN AIR

Plants act as highly effective air cleaners, absorbing carbon dioxide, plus many air pollutants, while releasing clean oxygen and fragrance.

RECYCLE

Recycling reduces the need to grow, harvest or extract new raw materials from the Earth, which provides less pollution of water, soil and air.

VEGETARIAN

Tends to consume less saturated fat and cholesterol and more Vitamin C, and dietary fiber. Start your 'GO GREEN" plan today

Include Environmental topics in your conversation.
Encourage practicing Safe environmental activities.

GLOSSARY

ACID RAIN

Rain or other forms of precipitation that is unusually acidic.

AIR POLLUTION

Air is made up of a number of gases, mostly nitrogen and oxygen and, in smaller amounts, water vapor, carbon dioxide and argon and other trace gases. Air pollution occurs when harmful chemicals and particles are emitted to the air – due to human activity or natural forces – at a concentration that interferes with human health or welfare or that harms the environment in other ways.

AQUIFER

A bed or layer yielding water for wells and springs etc.; an underground geological formation capable of receiving, storing and transmitting large quantities of water.

ATMOSPHERE

general name for the layer of gases around a material body; the Earth's atmosphere consists, from the ground up, of the troposphere (which includes the planetary boundary layer or peplosphere, the lowest layer), stratosphere, mesosphere, ionosphere (or thermosphere), exosphere and magnetosphere.

CRBON DIOXIDE

a colorless gas with the chemical formula CO_2, the most abundant greenhouse gas emitted from fossil fuels.

CARBON CREDIT

A unit of carbon dioxide bought to reduce greenhouse gas emissions. See carbon offset.

CARBON EMISSIONS

In the context of climate change, carbon dioxide released when substances, especially oil, gas, and coal, are burned by vehicles and planes, by factories and by homes.

CARBON FOOTPRINT
A measure of the impact our activities have on the
environment, especially climate change, often reported as
the units of tonnes (or kg) of carbon dioxide each of us
produces over a given period of time.
CARBON MONOXIDE
A highly poisonous, odourless, tasteless and colourless gas
that is formed when carbon material burns without enough
oxygen. Carbon monoxide is toxic when inhaled because it
combines with your blood and prevents oxygen from
getting to your organs. If a person is exposed to carbon
monoxide over a period, it can cause illness and even death.
Carbon Monoxide has no smell, taste or color. This is why
it is sometimes called the "Silent Killer". The most
common causes of carbon monoxide poisoning in the home
are house fires, faulty heating appliances such as boilers,
blocked chimney or flues, and rooms not properly
ventilated. Carbon Monoxide alarms can be used as a
backup to provide a warning to householders in the event of
a dangerous buildup of carbon monoxide.

CLIMATE CHANGE
A change in weather over time and/or region; usually
relating to changes in temperature, wind patterns and
rainfall; although may be natural or anthropogenic,
common discourse carries the assumption that climate
change is anthropogenic.

COMPOST
A rich soil-like material produced from decayed plants and
other organic matter, such as food and animal waste, that
decomposes (breaks down) naturally. Most food waste can
be put into compost, but you should not include meat,
bones, cheese, cooking oils and
fish. These may take a long time to break down and attract
unwanted pests.

DEFORESTATION

the conversion of forested areas to non-forest land for agriculture, urban use, development, or wasteland.

DRINKING WATER

(potable water) – water fit for human consumption in accordance with World Health Organization guidelines.

DROUGHT

An acute water shortage relative to availability, supply and demand in a particular region. An extended period of months or years when a region notes a deficiency in its water supply. Generally, this occurs when a region receives consistently below average precipitation.

DUMPING

Disposing of waste illegally by not using bins or official recycling centers, civic amenity sites or landfills.

ECOLOGY

the scientific study of living organisms and their relationships to one another and their environment.

ECOSYSTEM

A community of organisms that depend on each other and the environment they inhabit.

E-CYCLING

Recycling electronic waste.

ELECTRIC VEHICLE

A vehicle that is driven by an electric motor or battery and is generally less noisy and less polluting than common combustion engine vehicles.

EMISSIONS

Substances such as gases or particles discharged into the atmosphere as a result of natural processes of human activities, including those from chimneys, elevated point sources, and tailpipes of motor vehicles.

ENDANGERED SPECIES

A species which is at risk of becoming extinct because it is either few in number, or threatened by changing environmental or predation parameters.

ENVIRONMENT

The external conditions, resources, stimuli etc. with which an organism interacts.

EROSION

displacement of solids (sediment, soil, rock and other particles) usually by the agents of currents such as, wind, water, or ice by downward or down-slope movement in response to gravity or by living organisms.

E-WASTE

electronic waste, especially mobile phones, televisions and personal computers.

FERTILIZERS

compounds given to plants to promote growth; they are usually applied either through the soil, for uptake by plant roots, or by foliar feeding, for uptake through leaves.

FOSSIL FUEL

any hydrocarbon deposit that can be burned for heat or power, such as coal, oil and natural gas (produces carbon dioxide when burnt); fuels formed from once-living organisms that have become fossilized over geological time.

GREENHOUSE EFFECT

the process in which the emission of infrared radiation by the atmosphere warms a planet's surface.

GREENHOUSE GAS

components of the atmosphere that contribute to the greenhouse effect.

GROUND WATER

water located beneath the ground surface in soil pore spaces and in the fractures of lithologic formation.

GLOBAL DIMMING

A reduction in the amount of direct solar radiation reaching the surface of the earth due to light diffusion as a result of air pollution and increasing levels of cloud. A phenomenon of the last 30–50 years.

GLOBAL WARMING

the observable increase in global temperatures considered mainly caused by the human induced enhanced greenhouse effect trapping the Sun's heat in the Earth's atmosphere.

GREEN

(sustainability) like 'eco' - a word frequently used to indicate consideration for the environment e.g. green plumbers, green purchasing etc., sometimes used as a noun e.g. the Greens.

GREENHOUSE EFFECT

the insulating effect of atmospheric greenhouse gases (e.g., water vapor, carbon dioxide, methane, etc.) that keeps the Earth's temperature about 60 °F (16 °C) warmer than it would be otherwise cf. enhanced greenhouse effect.

GREENHOUSE GASES

any gas that contributes to the greenhouse effect; gaseous constituents of the atmosphere, both natural and from human activity, that absorb and re-emit infrared radiation. Water vapor (H_2O) is the most abundant greenhouse gas. Greenhouse gases are a natural part of the atmosphere and include carbon dioxide (CO_2), methane (CH_4, nitrous oxide, ozone (O_3), hydrofluorocarbons, perfluorocarbons and sulfur hexafluoride.

GREENLASH

dramatic changes in the structure and dynamic behavior of ecosystems.

GROUND WATER

Water that collects or flows underground in the small spaces in soil and rock. It might be a source of water for springs and wells and then used for drinking water.

HABITAT

an ecological or environmental area that is inhabited by a particular species.

HARD WASTE

household garbage which is not normally accepted into rubbish bins by local councils, e.g. old stoves, mattresses.

HEAT

energy derived from the motion of molecules; a form of energy into which all other forms of energy may be degraded.

HAZARDOUS WASTE

Waste that poses a risk to human health or the environment and needs to be handled and disposed of carefully. Examples include oil-based paints, car batteries, weed killers, bleach and waste electrical and electronic devices.

HOUSEHOLD WASTE

Waste that contains paper, cardboard, textiles (for example fabric or carpet), timber, food, garden clippings, glass, plastic and other manufactured materials.

HYDROCARBONS-

Chemicals made up of carbon and hydrogen that are found in raw materials such as petroleum, coal and natural gas, and derived products such as plastics.

LANDFILL

solid waste disposal in which refuse is buried between layers of soil, a method often used to reclaim low-lying ground; the word is sometimes used as a noun to refer to the waste itself.

LANDFILL GAS

the gas emissions from biodegrading waste in landfill, including CO.

Mulch--Leaves, straw or compost used to cover growing plants to protect them from the wind or cold.

MUNICIPAL WASTE

Waste produced in urban areas, mainly made up of household waste but also some small commercial waste that is similar to household waste.

NOISE POLLUTION-
Noises that disturb the environment and people's ability to enjoy it.

ORGANISM -Any living thing, from bacteria and fungi through to insects, plants, animals and humans.

OZONE LAYER
The thin protective layer of gas 10 to 50km above the Earth that acts as a filter for ultraviolet (UV) radiation from the sun. High UV levels can lead to skin cancer and cataracts and affect the growth of plants.

RADIATION
A form of energy that is transmitted in waves, rays or particles from a natural source, such as the sun and the ground, or an artificial source, such as an x-ray machine. Radiation can be IONIZING or non-IONIZING. IONIZING radiation includes ultraviolet rays, radon gas and X-rays. Too much exposure to IONIZING radiation can be harmful, leading to increased risk of cancer. Non-IONIZING radiation includes visible light, radio waves and microwaves. This type of radiation is less risky to health because it contains less energy, but it can still be harmful at high levels for a long time.

RADIOACTIVE
A material is said to be radioactive if it emits radiation.

RECYCLE
To break waste items down into their raw materials, which are then used to re-make the original item or make new items.

REFORESTATION-
The process of planting trees in forest lands to replace those that have been cut down.

REFUSE
Another name for waste.

RENEWABLE ENERGY
Energy from renewable resources such as wind power, solar energy or biomass.

RENEWABLE RESOURCE--A resource that can be used again and again without reducing its supply because it is constantly topped up, for example wind or sun rays.

REUSE

To use an item more than once for the same purpose, which helps save money, time, energy and resources.

SEWAGE

Liquid wastes from communities, which may be a mixture of domestic effluent from homes and liquid waste from industry.

SMOG

Air pollution consisting of smoke and fog, which occurs in large urban and industrial areas and is mainly caused by the action of sunlight on burned fuels, mostly from car exhausts. Smog can cause eye irritations and breathing problems and damage plant life.

SMOKELESS FUEL

Solid fuel, such as charcoal, that does not release smoke when it is burned.

SOLAR ENERGY

solar radiation used for hot water production and electricity generation (does not include passive solar energy to heat and cool buildings etc.);

SOLAR PANEL

A panel fixed to the roof of a building that uses special cells to collect energy from the sun and convert it to electricity to heat the building and/or power the lights, appliances or equipment.

SLUDGE

waste in a state between liquid and solid.

SUSTAINABILITY

Sustainable development is development that meets the needs of the present without compromising the ability of future generations to meet their own needs'.

TOXIC

Poisonous or harmful to the body (ecotoxic relates to damage to the environment).

TOXIN

A poisonous substance that can either be natural (produced by plants, animals or bacteria) or manufactured.

VENTILATION

In this guide, the movement of air between the inside and outside of a building usually through windows, doors and air vents built into the building's walls or ceilings.

WASTE -

any material (liquid, solid or gaseous) that is produced by domestic households and commercial, institutional, municipal or industrial organizations, and which cannot be collected and recycled in any way for further use. For solid wastes, this involves materials that currently go to landfills, even though some of the material is potentially recyclable.

WASTE MANAGEMENT

The management of waste collection, handling, processing, storage and transport from where it is produced to where it is finally disposed. See waste prevention.

WASTE PREVENTION

An aspect of waste management that involves reducing the amount of waste we produce and minimizing the potential harm to human health or the environment from packaging or ingredients in products.

WATER VAPOR

Water in its gas form – instead of liquid or solid (ice).

WIND ENERGY

Energy harnessed from the wind at wind farms and converted to power.

WIND TURBINE

An engine or machine, usually mounted on a towe, that captures the force of the wind and converts it to electricity.

ZERO EMISSIONS

An engine, motor or other energy source that does not produce any gas or release any harmful gases directly into the environment

ZERO WASTE

A set of principles focused on waste prevention that encourages redesigning resource life cycles so that all products are reused. The goal is to avoid sending trash to landfills, incinerators or dumped into the ocean.

NOTES:

HOW MUCH HAVE YOU

LEARNED ABOUT

GLOBAL WARMING AND

CLIMATE CHANGE?

TEST YOUR KNOWLEDGE

WITH THE

EVIRONMENTAL CROSS

WORDS AND QUIZ

MATCH COLUMN A WITH COLUMN B

COLUMN A

A.TRASH FLOATS BACK INTO THE OCEAN

B.TURN OFF WATER WHEN NOT IN USE

C. CROSS POLLINATION FRUITS AND VEGIABLES

D.LIFE OF PLANTS AND FISH LIVING IN THE OCEAN WATER

E.RE-USE OF TRASH

F.OCEAN MAMMALS DYEING FROM OCEAN POLLUTION

G.EARTH'S TEMPERATURE WARMING

H. CUTTING DOWN TREES

COLUMN B

1. **GLOBAL WARMING____**

2. **RECYLE___**

3. **PLASTIC POLLUTION____**

4. **DEFORESTATION____**

5. **WHAT IS TRASH___**

6. **CONSERVE WATER ____**

7. **HONEY BEES ___**

8. **ECO SYSTEMS ____**

9. **BEACH CLEAN IMORTANT___**

10. **CUT BACK ON PLASTIC BAGS_____**

EZ ENVIRONMENTAL CROSS WORDS

Down:

1. Rich soil like material produced from decayed plants, e-waste. electronic waste

2. A layer of gases around a material body, aquifer, a layer yielding water

3. An acute water shortage, dumping, disposing of waste

4. Any hydrocarbon deposit that can be burned for heat, global warming, increase in global temperatures

ARE WE
FOLLOWING THE
"GO GREEN"
PLANET EARTH
RESCUE MISSION
TO COMBAT
GLOBAL WARMING
AND
CLIMATE CHANGE
CONDITIONS?
VENUS

CAN WE KEEP OUR
GALAXY
CLEAN
FROM
TOXIC WASTE
DUMPING?
VENUS

ENJOY OTHER GREAT ENVIRONMENTAL BOOKS BY AUTHOR SANDI POPE.

The Veenus Environmental book series are educational and inspiring books that can be enjoyed by the entire family. They can also be used for homework, school work assignments, environmental projects and programs and more. You can start your VEENUS GREEN ACTION HERO collectible environmental library. All books are available on Amazon.com

https://www.amazon.com/author/sandipope4cistagirlveenus

Please feel free to visit our websites:

www.veenusecogirl.com

www.cista4cleanwater.com

Contact: Sandi Pope

cista4cleanwater@gmail.com

View cista girl's history at a glance: www.cista4cleanwater.com

Facebook page Veenus Eco Girl

You Tube Veenus Eco Girl

Cista Girl R
VEENUS
GREEN ACTION HERO
THE EFFECTS OF
GLOBAL WARMING
BY SANDI POPE

CISTA GIRL VEENUS GREEN ACTION HERO, EFFECTS OF GLOBAL WARMING"

This book —The Effects of Global Warming‖ provides important details about the cause and effects of global warming. It shares how humans are the major cause of global warming and it also shares how we can build health and wellness and build a healthy planet too.

 It's also important to know how global warming and climate change will affect our next generation. It's also important to take action now, to reduce global warming and climate change conditions.

It's also important to understand that climate change is becoming more active, and what and how to prepare for conditions that may become overwhelming. Due to the past and increasingly devastating hurricanes, wild fires and ocean swells, we can no longer guess about natural conditions that have now become devastating conditions to our communities and lifestyles. The following books that include a brief description should ignite you to purchase the books to learn more about climate change and build your environmental library as well. Take action now to reduce global warming conditions.

BE AWARE. FOLLOW VEENUS "SAVE OUR PLANET GO GREEN" ENJOY YOUR BOOKS. START YOUR ENVIRONMENTAL LIBRARY TODAY.

https://www.amazon.com/author/sandipope4cistagirlveenus

Cista Girl R
VEENUS
GREEN ACTION HERO
SAVE OUR PLANET
PLANT MORE TREES
BY SANDI POPE

CISTA GIRL VEENUS GREEN ACTION HERO "SAVE OUR PLANET, PLANT MORE TREES"

This is an excellent book that shares the very important history about trees. The history of trees is fascinating because trees did not look like trees in their past history. There are thousands of unique species of trees all over the planet crying out to reduce global warming and climate change so they can survive. We take trees for granted because they are always there, but due to wild fires and droughts as the result of climate change, trees are quickly diminishing. The great important information about this book is that it can teach you how to start the life a tree, right on you window sill or in your backyard or garden. Trees are so vital for the health of humans because in their structure they suck in toxic air and give us clean air. to breath. . Deforestation has had a major impact on the reduction of trees and the stability of tree life. Because you see trees in your local park or on your block does not mean we have reached the goal of not planting more trees. On the contrary, we use trees for so many things that satisfy our need for different kinds of products. That's why it's important to consider starting a —plant a tree project‖ in your community. **FOLLOW VEENUS "SAVE OUR PLANET, PLANT MORE TREES" ENJOY YOUR BOOKS. START YOUR ENVIRONMENTAL LIBRARY TODAY.**

https://www.amazon.com/author/sandipope4cistagirlveenus

Cista Girl R
VEENUS
GREEN ACTION HERO
SAVE OUR PLANET
"LETS TALK TRASH"
BY SANDI POPE

CISTA GIRL VEENUS GREEN ACTION HERO "SAVE OUR PLANET, LET'S TALK TRASH"

This is an excellent book that shares the very important history about, TRASH. How trash is accumulated and how it negatively impacts our environment. We must be aware that trash is one of the major components that ignite global warming and climate conditions. This is a great book because it identifies all kinds of trash, how it starts to build up, what to do with it and how to remove it. This book also identifies who and what are the highest producers of trash. Where trash is being dumped and why. Do you know just how harmful trash is to our environment? Trash can be used in very useful ways but most often in devastating ways. We as humans must learn that trash as a key contributor to global warming, how to reduce the makings of trash and the best way to dispose of trash. Trash can not only cause fires but can also contribute to disease and the spread of very unhealthy conditions. We must learn how to identify trash and how to dispose of trash correctly. We must begin to feel comfortable dividing our trash and disposing trash into the proper recycle bins in order to reduce the devastating conditions of climate change. Take a look around your lifestyle and see if you have excess trash. Trash can be people, places and things. **FOLLOW VEENUS "SAVE OUR PLANET, LET'S TALK TRASH" ENJOY YOUR BOOKS. START YOUR ENVIRONMENTAL BOOK LIBRARY TODAY.**

Cista Girl™
VEENUS
GREEN ACTION HERO
SAVE OUR PLANET
SAVE OUR CHILDREN
BY SANDI DORE

CISTA GIRL VEENUS GREEN ACTION HERO "SAVE OUR PLANET SAVE OUR CHILDREN"

An essential book that will bring awareness to how our children "to be" will play an important role in the Climate change crisis. Our "to be" children are often fed the best stuff to build a strong and healthy mind and body. Until the age of 5, when they begin to make some decisions about some things, parents have a choice then to help them make decisions that will help them lead the way to save the planet. Those decisions are choices that will grow into a child's heart and soul and will help them build health and wellness for their own body and build health and wellness in the soul of planet earth. As leaders in the next generation they will have to be aware that the decisions they make now will directly support the building a healthy planet where they will live. or a devastating planet that will be unforgiving. Children at 12 years old should be knowledgeable of the cause and effects of global warming and how it will affect them, their community, their friends and family.This is a great book to read and study to acquire the essence of the material. Most importantly how to apply the information to accomplished planned goals for a dynamic outcome. A good read for the entire family. **FOLLOW VEENUS "SAVE OUR PLANET SAVE OUR CHILDREN. ENJOY YOUR BOOKS. START YOUR ENVIRONMENTAL BOOK LIBRARY TODAY**

Cista Girl R
VEENUS
GREEN ACTION HERO
YOUR
"GO GREEN"
GUIDE
TO START
A HOME BASE
BUSINESS
PART I
HOW TO BE IN YOUR
BEST HEALTH
BY SANDI POPE

CISTA GIRL VEENUS GREEN ACTION HERO "YOUR GO GREEN GUIDE TO START A HOME BASED BUSINESS PT I HOW TO BE IN YOUR BEST HEALTH"

This is a very important and helpful book for entrepreneurs. In order to feed and take care of your newly formed business or an established business that will require your attention 24/7, you must be in your best health. This book promotes the Feng Shui method to help develop your best health lifestyle. Feng Shui is famous for organizing, restructuring and identifying habits that are not useful or healthy to contribute to a healthy living condition. Our habits can get in the way of healthy productivity. Feng Shui takes you from room to room in your living space and shares with you how each room affects your health. This is a great book to explore, to help you identify a new positive way of operating your business in your home and how to make the change. This book will also encourage ways to remake your old business to a healthy GO GREEN BUSINESS. This book will also help you seek out new GO GREEN Clients that may have been overlooked because there was no interest at that time. So get ready to let Feng Shui take over your lifestyle and prepare you for great changes. Remember to take tiny steps first to see your progress. Review and assess your progress to get a —good fit‖ feel. Then you can move on to the next step. Remember, trying to establish a GO GREEN home base business, Feng Shui will definitely help build your health and wellness that will directly help with the wellness of planet earth.
FOLLOW VEENUS "YOUR GO GREEN GUIDE TO START A HOME BASE BUSINESS" PART I, HOW TO BE IN YOUR BEST HEALTH. ENJOY YOUR BOOKS. START YOUR ENVIRONMENTAL BOOK LIBRARY TODAY.

Cista Girl R
VEENUS
GREEN ACTION HERO
YOUR
"GO GREEN"
GUIDE
TO START
A HOME BASE
BUSINESS
PART II
ACTIVATE YOUR
"GO GREEN" BUSINESS
By Sandi Pope

"YOUR GO GREEN GUIDE TO START A HOME BASE BUSINESS PT II, HOW TO ACTIVATE YOUR GO GREEN BUSINESS"

This is a great book that continues from Part I. Now that you are in your best health you can begin to activate your business. The enormous benefit of being in your best health will stand by your energy when your business becomes very demanding. These demands may be 24/7 but you'll be prepared. This book also energizes you to explore new GREEN ideas that may excel your business to another level. This book also helps you assess how to —Activate‖ your business. FENG SHUI will help with organization and focus is the key. This book is not one to read all at once. It is a reference guide that you visit from time to time to upgrade your ideas, change a plan, include or expand your GO GREEN ideas. To Activate your business is a long term commitment and goal. It's important to stay focus to cover your main goal and objective. Once you are organized, and it may take some time, you can begin to understand and apply activation, and FENG SHUI will definitely be a factor in your success and activation plan. **FOLLOW VEENUS "YOUR GO GREEN GUIDE TO START A HOME BASE BUSINESS" PART II, ACTIVATE YOUR HOME BASE BUSINESS. ENJOY YOUR BOOKS. START YOUR ENVIRONMENTAL BOOK LIBRARY TODAY** .https://www.amazon.com/author/sandipope4cistagirlveenus

Cista Girl R
VEENUS
GREEN ACTION HERO
SAVE OUR PLANET
SAVE OUR BUTTERFLIES
BY SANDI POPE

CISTA GIRL VEENUS GREEN ACTION HERO "SAVE OUR PLANET SAVE OUR BUTTERFLIES"

A great book that will bring awareness to the lifestyles of butterflies. The butterfly is a fascinating insect. One of the most beautiful with one of the most alluring lifestyles. We see the fluttering beauty, here and there in our gardens and parks. That fluttering has a specific meaning. We see butterflies in a variety of colors and that too has significant meanings. This book explores the lifecycle of butterflies and brings awareness, that it is the only insect on planet earth that goes through a mystical life changes called METAMORPHOSIS. We should be aware of the importance of insects, like the butterflies and bees that have specific meaning to their lives on the planet. Butterflies and bees are pollinators that carry life from one flower or plant to another that gives us life. Without bees and butterflies life would cease to exist on the planet. So butterflies are extremely important. This book suggests ways to attract butterflies in your garden and even start a project or program to bring awareness about butterflies. Learn more about the history of butterflies. **FOLLOW VEENUS "SAVE OUR PLANET SAVE OUR BUTTERFLIES" ENJOY YOUR BOOKS. START YOUR ENVIRONMENTAL BOOK LIBRARY TODAY.**
https://www.amazon.com/author/sandipope4cistagirlveenus

Veenus Eco Girl
GREEN ACTION HERO
REUSE
REDUCE
RENEW
RECYCLE
SAVE OUR PLANET
"GO GREEN"
BY SANDI POPE
VEENUS ECO GIRL
GREEN ACTION HERO

CISTA GIRL VEENUS GREEN ACTION HERO "SAVE OUR PLANET, GO GREEN"

This is an excellent book that shares 12 GO GREEN steps to include in your daily lifestyle that will make a big impact in building your health and wellness and a healthy planet too. Go Green means to live a sustainable life, that will help maintain the overall health of yourself and the planet. The planet will only be as healthy as the humans that live on the planet. So it is essential for humans to participate in a way that will first, build their own health and wellness and then —planet good health‖ will follow. The 12 GO GREEN steps are to use to follow weekly programs that can be included in your daily lifestyle. Don‗t forget that planet earth, due to our habits is going through enormous crisis and is crying out for help. We cannot ignore the outcome of devastating hurricanes. We cannot ignore the outbursts and results of wild fires that burn millions of acres or good earth. We can set a path for recovery by including a GO GREEN lifestyle into our everyday lives. We have to start somewhere to make a change to reduce climate change conditions. To begin, you can recycle, reduce, reuse and renew as part of the GO GREEN mission. **BE AWARE. FOLLOW VEENUS "SAVE OUR PLANET GO GREEN" ENJOY YOUR BOOKS. START YOUR ENVIRONMENTAL LIBRARY TODAY.**

https://www.amazon.com/author/sandipope4cistagirlveenus

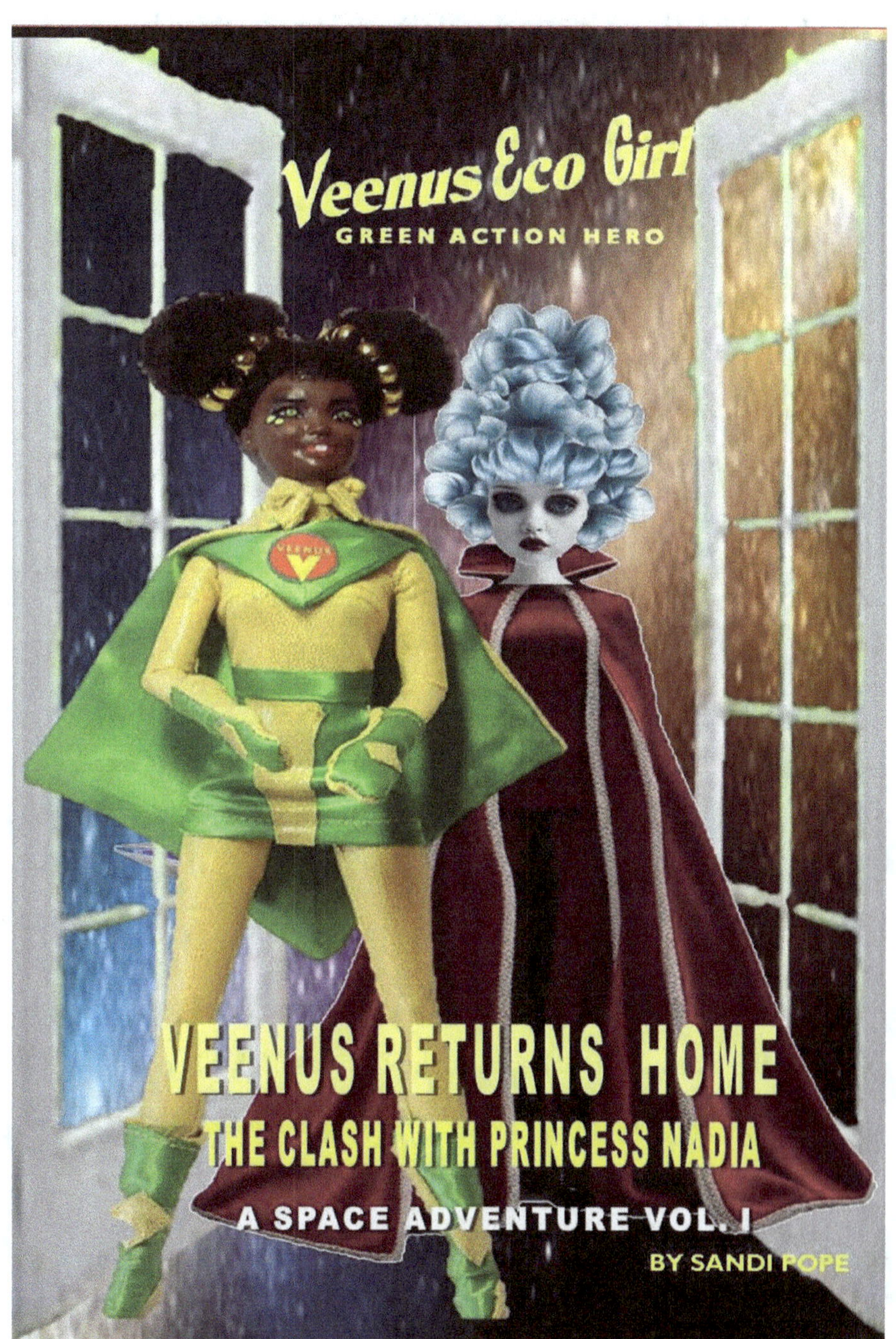
Veenus Eco Girl
GREEN ACTION HERO
VEENUS RETURNS HOME
THE CLASH WITH PRINCESS NADIA
A SPACE ADVENTURE VOL. I
BY SANDI POPE

91

CISTA GIRL VEENUS IS NOW MORE POWERFUL AS VEENUS ECO GIRL GREEN ACTION HERO. " VEENUS RETURNS HOME, CLASH WITH PRINCESS NADIA"

This book shares the history of Veenus, how she became a Green Action Hero and was given the mission to save the Veenushia Galaxy and keep it safe and clean. Veenus is commissioned to save another planet in the Veenushia Galaxy and during the time away from her

planet —Venus‖ it was invaded by Princess Nadia. The fearless ambition of Princess Nadia is to take over the Veenushia Galaxy to gain Universal power. Venus has plans to rebuild planet Venus but continue to be distracted by Princess Nadia. Along with the challenges with Princess Nadia, Veenus discovers hidden mountains and caves with captured slaves held by Princess Nadia where she finds her family.

Find out more how Princess Nadia challenges Veenus to take over the Veenushia Galaxy and the Universe. This book is similar to our everyday lives of Power, Greed and the fight for survival. **FOLLOW VEENUS "VEENUS RETURNS HOME, CLASH WITH PRINCESS NADIA. ENJOY YOUR BOOKS. START YOUR ENVIRONMENTAL BOOK LIBRARY TODAY.**

https://www.amazon.com/author/sandipope4cistagirlveenus

Veenus Eco Girl
GREEN ACTION HERO
VEENUS
THE
METAMORPHOSIS
OF VEENUS
THE CAPTURE OF THE SPACE CRIMINAL PRINCESS NADIA
BY SANDI POPE

VEENUS ECO GIRL IS NOW THE NEW MORE POWERFUL GREEN ACTION HERO. "THE METAMORPHOSIS OF VEENUS, THE CAPTURE OF PRINCESS NADIA" VOL II

This book is an exciting adventure continued from PT I, where Veenus continues on the path to capture Princess Nadia and King Nordic, and expunge them from the universe for good. Veenus had to go through a Metamorphosis to get more power to capture the Nordic Team. As the universe and galaxy are endless, it was easy for the Nordic team to escape and hide and build a fighting force. Princess Nadia is focused on distracting Veenus in any way to take over the Veenushia Galaxy to gain universal power. Veenus had to go through very serious steps and commitment to be in the stage of the Metamorphosis. Rules and very strong irreversible guidelines are set in stages of the Metamorphosis. In order for Veenus to maintain her super powers she must obey the rules without question. Find out what happens as Veenus may have disobeyed the rules of the Metamorphosis. **FOLLOW VEENUS "THE METAMORPHOSIS OF VEENUS, THE CAPTURE OF SPACE CRIMINAL PRINCESS NADIA" ENJOY YOUR BOOKS. START YOUR ENVIRONMENTAL LIBRARY TODAY.**

https://www.amazon.com/author/sandipope4cistagirlveenus

Cista Girl R
VEENUS
GREEN ACTION HERO
BUTTERFLIES
COLORING BOOK
KIDS AND ADULTS
BY SANDI POPE

Veenus Eco Girl
GREEN ACTION HERO
REUSE
REDUCE
RENEW
RECYCLE
SAVE OUR PLANET
"LET'S GO GREEN"
COLORING BOOK
KIDS AND ADULTS
BY SANDI POPE